Strange Animals

Strange Animals

TOM JACKSON

amber
BOOKS

Published by Amber Books Ltd
United House
North Road
London
N7 9DP
United Kingdom
www.amberbooks.co.uk
Instagram: amberbooksltd
Facebook: amberbooks
Twitter: @amberbooks
Pinterest: amberbooksltd

ISBN: 978-1-83886-282-4

Project Editor: Michael Spilling
Designer: Keren Harragan
Picture Research: Justin Willsdon

Printed in China

Contents

Introduction

Perhaps the strangest thing about animals is that there are any of them at all! However, the natural miracle of life means there are at least 1.5 million types of animal on Earth, found everywhere from deep-sea vents to bone-dry deserts. Animals do not extract the energy and nutrients they need to survive directly from the non-living air, soil and water of the biosphere; they leave that job to other life forms, mostly plants, which animals eat – along with other animals – to stay alive.

Strange animals are those that live in unusual ways. This book takes a broad view, looking at the different animals groups – some cute, and some not so much – and picking out a particularly distinctive species. So, instead of the grey wolf, keep an eye out for the red wolf, and instead of the jaguar, look for a jaguarundi. Along the way, we'll also see some uniquely strange creatures, such as the tuataras of New Zealand, which were once neighbours of early dinosaurs, and the axolotls of Mexico, water monsters that never grow up.

ABOVE:
Aardwolf
The aardwolf of southern Africa is no wolf at all, but a type of hyena that eats ants and termites – as many as a quarter of a million of them in one meal!

OPPOSITE:
Musk ox
This hairy Arctic beast looks like a buffalo or bison, but in fact this young musk ox is the largest member of the sheep family. Musk oxen spend the winter out in the open and are protected from the wind by the longest hairs in the animal kingdom.

Asia

The largest continent has more than its fair share of strange animals. Its territory stretches from the Arctic wastes in the north to the sultry south seas. This area includes the world's largest forest; the taigas of northern Asia span about a quarter of the globe. To the south, the steppes of Central Asia are also the world's largest grasslands. To top it all, Asia has some of the most diverse rainforests on the globe, which extend both sides of the Equator, not to mention the multiple wetlands, mountains and deserts. In short, there are a lot of different places for animals to live in Asia, and some of them do it in strange ways.

Take the tarsiers. These are primates, and so relatives of us humans. They occupy their own group, and are neither monkey nor ape, bushbaby nor lemur. A tarsier is an insect-hunter, barely 12 cm (4.7 in) tall, with long hands for climbing through the trees. It is active at night, working in the safety of darkness, and so to find its prey it needs highly sensitive vision. That is why tarsiers have the biggest eyes relative to their body size of any mammal. Each of the eyeballs is bigger than the brain!

The tarsiers are just the beginning. Asia is also home to gazelles with giant nostrils, the world's biggest hornet, a crocodile that buzzes underwater, and so much more.

OPPOSITE:
Tarsier
This wide-eyed primate likes to sit motionless in the dark forest before ambushing any insects that clamber past.

ABOVE:
Colugo
A baby colugo peers out from the safety of its mother's arms. Her limbs are connected by a membrane of skin. Despite appearances, that skin is not there to serve as a swaddling blanket but rather as a wing-like surface, which this unusual mammal from the forests of Southeast Asia uses to glide from tree to tree.

OPPOSITE:
A flying lemur?
The colugo is also called the Sunda flying lemur, although it is not a true lemur, since those are primates confined to Madagascar. The nocturnal forest herbivore is, however, a close cousin of the primates, and both groups probably shared a common ancestor about 70 million years ago.

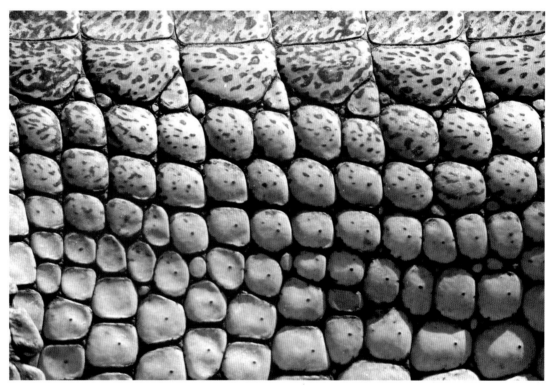

LEFT:
Gharial
This crocodile from South Asia is long – as long as any crocodile – but very slender. It does not trouble large animals, but uses its long, toothy snout to snatch fish from river water. The males have a 'pot' on the snout, which makes a deep buzzing call underwater.

ABOVE TOP:
Gharial eye
The gharial's eye has a mirrored layer behind the retina, which reflects light back on to sensors so the animal can see better in the dark. There are also see-through membranes that sweeps sideways over the eyes. These work like goggles to protect the eyes under water.

ABOVE BOTTOM:
Gharial skin
River water is often dark, and so the gharial uses super-sensitive touch organs in its scaly skin to pick up the swirls and ripples made in the water by fish swimming nearby.

LEFT:
Giant hornet

The Asian giant hornet, which is found across East Asia and has recently spread to North America, is the world's largest hornet. It grows to 4.5 cm (1.7 in) long and has a wingspan of 7.5 cm (3 in). Its sting is 6 mm (0.2 in) long – four times the length of a honeybee's! Stings hurt but are not particularly dangerous to humans unless the recipient is allergic.

ABOVE:
Giant hornets' nest

These big insects live in relatively small colonies containing fewer than 100 workers. A new queen sets up her colony in April, raises the first generation of workers and then continues to lay eggs through the summer and into September.

ALL PHOTOGRAPHS:
Golden snub-nosed monkey
With its blue face and mane of orange fur, this Chinese species
does not conform to the normal monkey looks. It lives in the cold
mountain forests of central China, gathering in rowdy gangs, in which
disagreements are frequent. Actual fights are generally averted by males
showing off their main weapons – their long teeth.

Honey badger
Also called the ratel, this fierce mammal lives in sub-Saharan Africa and across southern Asia. The creature earns its name from its love of honey (and bee larvae). It searches for nests and rips them open with its long claws. The thick skin makes the badger impervious to stings.

Leaf insect

On closer inspection, this ragged leaf is in fact a camouflaged insect with six legs and a head with a pair of eyes and small, stubby antennae. Leaf insects are found in forested areas from South Asia to Australia. Those that live in the branches of living trees are green, while those on the forest floor match the darker colours of rotting leaves.

Japanese macaque

Few monkeys face winter snows. The Japanese macaque is one of the few types that does, and is the northernmost species in the world. As winter hits, most of these so-called snow monkeys head south, but a few living in the mountains around Nagano are able to stay where they are and keep warm by taking a dip in hot springs.

Mekong freshwater stingray
These stingrays, which live in the Mekong River and other river systems in Southeast Asia, are among the largest freshwater fish in the world. Some will grow to 3 m (9.8 ft) from snout to tail tip. The tail carries spines that are reportedly thick enough to cut through wooden fishing boats.

ALL PHOTOGRAPHS:
Komodo dragon
With a name that is no exaggeration, this is the largest lizard on Earth. It lives on the island of Komodo and a few more neighbouring islands in central Indonesia. At 3 m (9.8 ft) long, this fierce predator takes on big prey, such as buffalo, pigs and smaller Komodo dragons. The dragon's saliva contains a venom that subdues prey and causes the bite to rapidly become infected. The dragon then tracks its big victims as they steadily weaken over several days.

Saiga

This is an unusual relative of the gazelles, although it is a bit more sturdy and short-legged than its cousins. The saiga lives in herds in Central Asia but has been hunted close to extinction for its horns. It has enormous, hairy nostrils, which filter dust in the dry season, and warm cold air entering the lungs in winter.

Raccoon dog
It may look like a raccoon, an American generalist, but this northeast Asian mammal belongs to the dog family. It lives in small family groups in dense forests.

Sloth bear
This bear, which is found throughout South Asia, earns its name from its shaggy coat, which reminds people of sloths, especially since the bear sometimes hangs upside down from branches using its long claws to grip on. Those claws are mostly used to rip apart the nests of ants and termites – the bear's favourite food – which it sucks up using its long lower lip and palate.

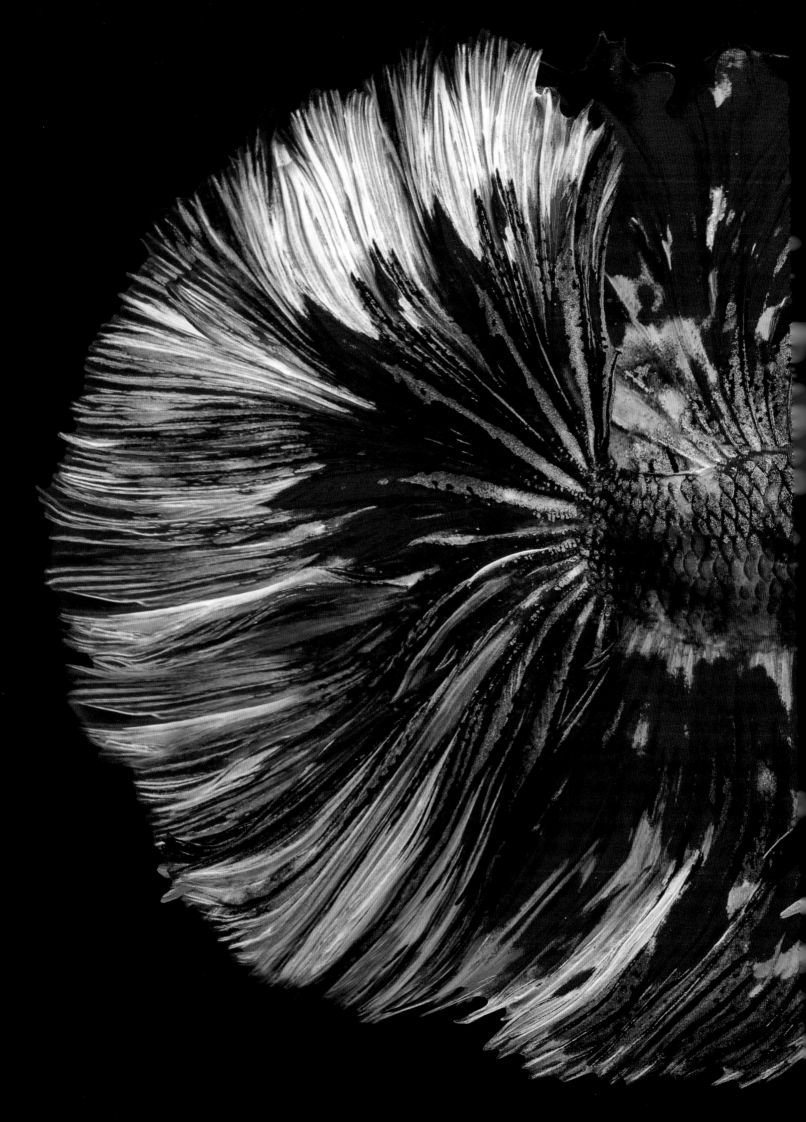

LEFT:

Siamese fighting fish

This freshwater fish is a type of betta that is found in the wild across eastern Asia. It lives in slow-flowing water and can survive in low-oxygen environments. The wild types lack the colouring of captive fish. The long fins allow them to orientate themselves in still water as they slowly patrol a territory. The fish will always fight when two of them end up in one territory – hence the name.

ABOVE TOP AND BOTTOM:

Siberian sturgeon

This type of fish, which is found in the Lena, Yenisei and Ob river systems, is exceptional for living for up to 60 years. Along with all species of sturgeon, this massive river fish is in grave peril of extinction since it is killed for its roe, or eggs, which grow internally. These eggs are cut out of the dead adult and made into caviar.

Malayan tapir
A tapir mother and her young
calf rest on the forest floor. When
on the move again, this chunky
creature uses its wedge-shaped
body, wider at the rump, to drive
itself through the jungle at night.

Tapir feet
The tapir is a relative of the horse
and rhino. It has three toes, each
tipped with a hoof on the back
feet and four toes at the front.

Tapir snout
The flexible snout, or proboscis,
is the tapir's defining feature. It
evolved independently of those
of elephants, which are only very
distant relatives. The proboscis
is used to pluck leaves and fruits
from bushes.

Tokay

This is the world's largest gecko species. It grows to around 35 cm (14 in) from snout to tail tip. That large size does not stop the gecko from using adhesive pads on its clawed toes to stick to smooth surfaces as it climbs. The predatory gecko is named after the sound of its distinctive call.

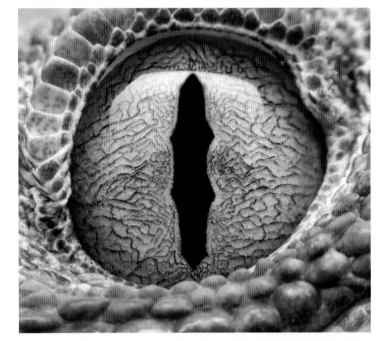

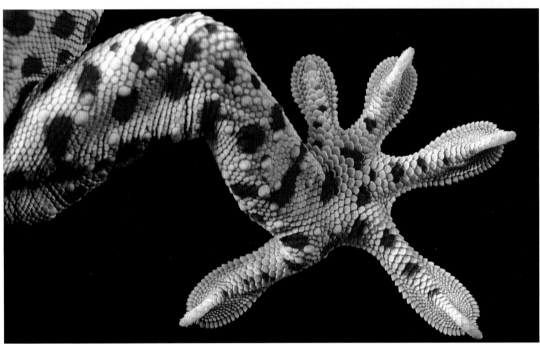

ALL PHOTOGRAPHS:
Mudskipper
A fish that breathes air is nothing if not strange. The mudskippers, which live around the coasts of the Indian Ocean and western Pacific, breathe underwater with the usual arrangement of gills. However, since they prey on small crustaceans that are found in mud, the fish haul themselves on to mudflats – or leap and skip up the shore – and breathe oxygen directly through the skin while out of the water.

ALL PHOTOGRAPHS:

Proboscis monkey
Borneo's famous big-nosed monkey lives in the coastal mangrove swamps. It is the adult males that are blessed with large noses, which serve as a signal of their virility and general health. There is no other species that looks anything like it.

Zarudny's worm lizard
One look at a Zarudny's worm lizard squirming on the desert sands of the Middle East might lead to confusion. The worm part of its name makes sense, but why lizard? This creature is an amphisbaenian, a relative of the lizards that has lost its legs to adopt a subterranean lifestyle eating grubs and earthworms.

Slow loris
This cute character is a nocturnal primate of the Southeast Asian forests. It climbs through the branches in a comedic slow motion, its aim being to never attract attention from predators that are primed to pick up sudden movements in the dark. The loris repeatedly licks a gland on its arm. This mixes a toxin into the saliva, which makes a bite from a loris very unpleasant. Mammal predators soon learn to avoid them.

Africa

The second largest continent is dominated by tropical habitats ranging from deserts to jungles. It contains the Sahara, the largest desert on Earth, which is surprisingly full of life. One of the biggest wild animals to live there is the addax, an antelope that never needs to drink water. Africa is also home to the Congo Basin, a patchwork of lush rainforests that grows around the second biggest river in the world. Chimpanzees and gorillas are found there, as well as a host of stranger creatures, such as the okapi, a mysterious relative of the giraffe; the gaboon viper, a snake with a few very big claims to fame; and the mandrill, the world's biggest monkey species. Male mandrills are much bigger than the females – in fact,

they are too large to climb very high off the forest floor. They have given up that ability in favour of strength and power, attributes they consolidate with lurid colouring of reds and blues. To demonstrate just how tough they are, they yawn aggressively, showing off long fangs.

Africa's most famous animals live on the savannah grasslands. Among the lions, hippos and elephants, some strange species make a life, including the aardvark, gerenuk and a fish that survives when rivers run dry.

Finally, across the Mozambique Channel is Madagascar, an island with perhaps the strangest collection of animals of all. It is well known for its lemurs, but there are also bizarre insects, minute lizards, and a top predator that's like nothing else on Earth.

OPPOSITE:
Mandrill
The facial colouring of a mandrill becomes brighter and more obvious when the monkey becomes excited. You can't say that you weren't warned!

Tough guy
This mighty monkey is from the Congo rainforest. Male mandrills grow to 1 m (3.3 ft) tall and weigh 30 kg (66 lb) – and they are tough with it. The colourful face and fur are a signal that this guy is not to be messed around with. Only an animal as healthy and strong as he could risk looking this strange. So, watch out!

LEFT:

Armadillo girdled lizard

This South African lizard looks well-armoured with its overlapping plate-like scales. However, the little reptile – it's about 15 cm (6 in) long – takes an extra precaution when threatened, looping its body around into a circle, a little like the ball some armadillos form. This defensive posture protects the soft underbelly from injury.

OVERLEAF LEFT:

Giraffe weevil

This Malagasy insect looks too strange to be true but it is an example of extreme sexual dimorphism. Only the males have such a long neck – which is three times the length of that of the females. The neck is a signal of its health and status and is used in fights over mates.

OVERLEAF RIGHT:

Hammer-headed bat

This species is the largest bat living on the African mainland. It has a wingspan of just under 1 m (3.3 ft). The fruit-eater is said to be a 'hammer-headed' because the male has a highly enlarged snout housing a cavity that is used to amplify mating calls.

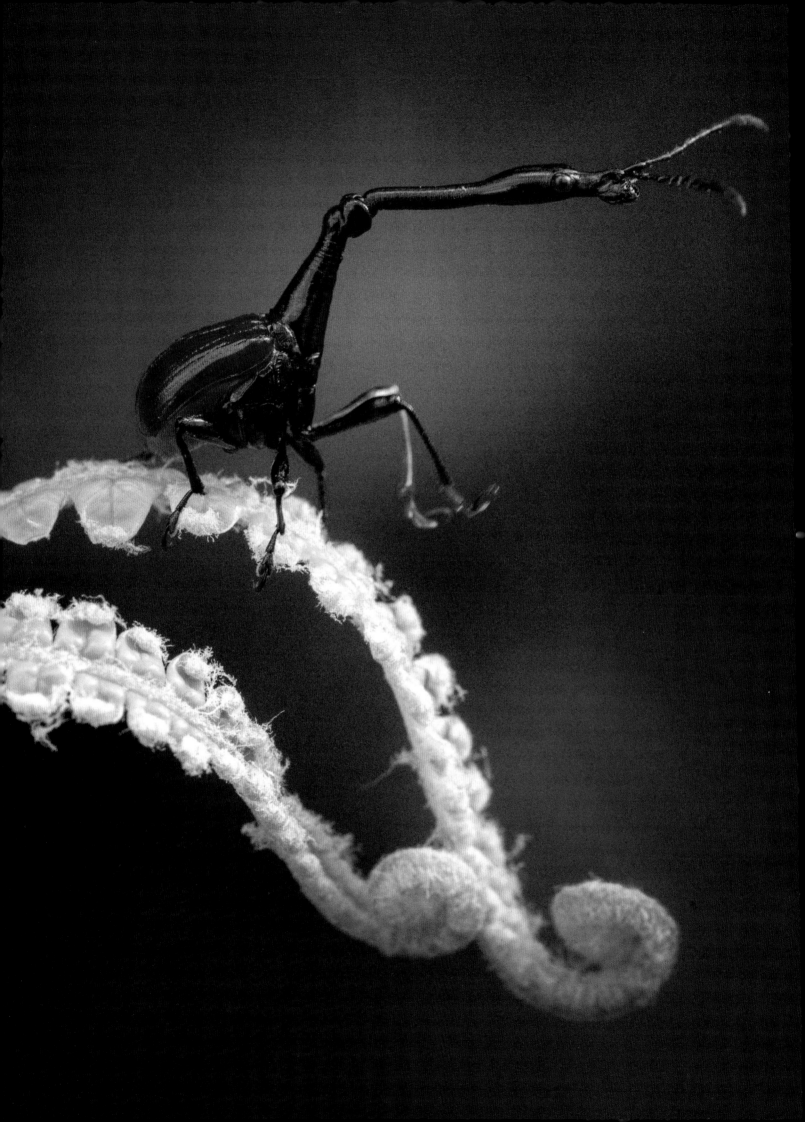

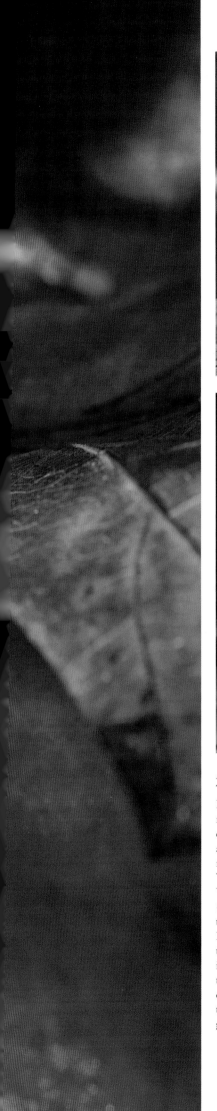

ALL PHOTOGRAPHS:
Tomato frog
It might seem an unnecessary
risk for this frog to be so brightly
coloured. It certainly stands out
among the moss and herbs of its
rainforest home on Madagascar.
The red is actually a warning.
When threatened, the 8 cm
(3.1 in)-long frog puffs itself up
to seem bigger than it really is.
If a predator is not deterred by
that and grabs the tomato frog in
its mouth, it soon discovers that
the red skin is covered in a layer
of toxic slime. The liquid makes
the predator's face go numb. It
generally lets the frog go after that.

Gaboon viper
This venomous snake from Central Africa holds a few records. It has the longest fangs of any snake; they can be 5 cm (2 in) long. It also delivers the most venom per bite, and one bite can kill a human. However, bites are rare. Instead, this chunky snake, the heaviest venomous snake of all (reaching as much as 20 kg/44 lb), tends to lie motionless in the leaves, waiting to ambush prey.

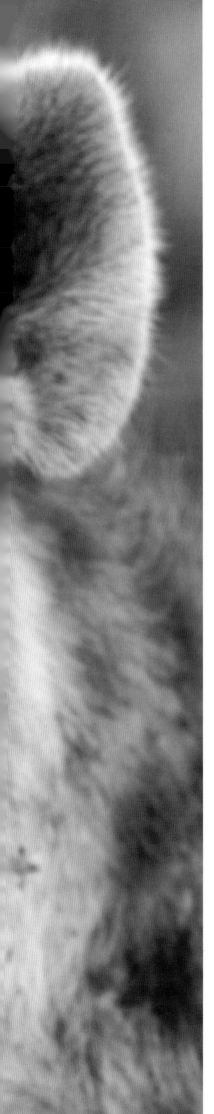

ALL PHOTOGRAPHS:
Spotted hyena
Hyenas are strange carnivores. They look like a halfway house between big cats and wild dogs. In fact, they are a rough and tough cousin of the mongooses. This spotted species is the biggest. It is a scavenger on the plains of Africa, and has a bite strong enough to crack bone and reach the nutritious marrow within. Spotted hyenas live in clans ruled by dominant females.

ALL PHOTOGRAPHS:
Gerenuk
Confined to the arid grasslands of the Horn of Africa, this gazelle seems too slender for its own good. The long legs and neck make the gerenuks fast runners but also agile enough to stand up on their back legs (and lean on the forelegs), so they can reach up to eat fresh leaves and fruits.

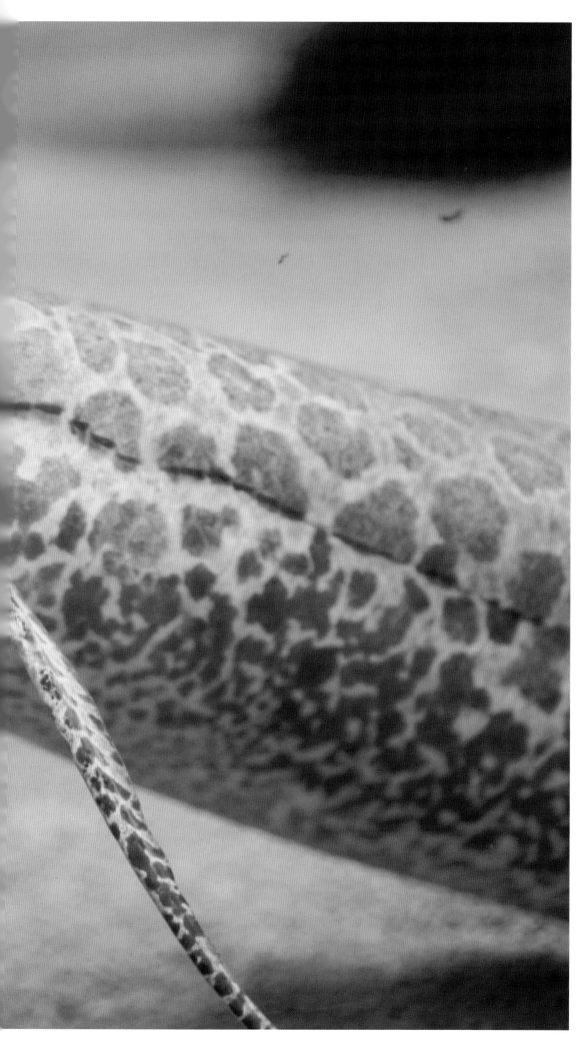

African lungfish
These eel-like fish live in shallow streams and ponds in tropical Africa, where there is often not much oxygen in the warm water. To compensate, they take gulps of air at the surface and oxygen is absorbed by a rudimentary lung. Inevitably, the water dries out entirely from time to time. The fish creates a waterproof bag of skin and mucus around it and waits in the deep mud for the rains to return.

RIGHT TOP AND BOTTOM:
Nano chameleon
This Malagasy lizard cannot
change colour like its cousins from
further abroad, but it makes up for
that by being among the smallest
reptiles on the planet, measuring
22 mm (0.9 in) from its snout to
the tip of its tail.

OPPOSITE:
Okapi
A tall and mysterious forest beast,
the okapi is the closest living
relative to the giraffe. It browses
leaves using its long tongue,
but has no need for a long neck
because there are plenty of fresh
leaves within easy reach in the
Congo rainforests.

OPPOSITE BOTH PHOTOGRAPHS:
Okapi bone spikes
Like the giraffe, the okapi has ossicones, which are bone spikes on the head covered in skin. In this way, they resemble horns, although ossicones have a permanent covering of skin or fur rather than keratin, and develop in a different way to horns.

ABOVE AND LEFT:
Naked mole-rat
The semideserts of southwestern Africa are a tough place to live. One answer is to team up to survive. Naked mole-rats are burrowing mammals that have adopted the same social structure as ants and termites. A single queen mole-rat breeds, and then controls her workers using chemicals in her urine.

BELOW:
African hoopoe
This distinctive bird is a resident cousin of a very similar Eurasian species that migrates back to East Africa to spend the winter. This species lives all year round in southern Africa, preying on insects. It is famed for its 'oop-oop' call, which earned it its name.

OPPOSITE:
Tree pangolin
This nocturnal pangolin is climbing up a tree trunk heading back for a sleep in a hollow higher up. The pangolin uses its clawed feet to walk straight up the bark. Once in the treetops, the long, prehensile tail serves as a fifth limb, helping the pangolin to grab branches.

Armoured anteater
It looks like a reptile, but the pangolin – also called the scaly anteater – is actually a mammal. Look closely, and you will find bristled hairs between the horny scales that cover the body. The pangolin has an immensely long tongue – a third of the whole body length – which licks up insects at lightning speed.

ALL PHOTOGRAPHS:
Marabou stork
This large, lumbering wading
bird is a scavenger. Its dark,
cloak-like plumage and hunched
demeanour have earned it the
nickname the 'undertaker bird'.
It stalks the grasslands of Africa,
especially areas close to rivers and
lakes, searching for carrion. It will
also catch live prey, such as fish
and lizards.

Aye-aye

In the dead of night, this bizarre lemur is hard at work. It taps branches with its long ring finger. It is listening for sounds of hollows under the bark, which would indicate a chubby woodworm or grub is burrowing there. It then digs out the treat with its long claws.

African fat-tailed gecko

A camel has a hump, whereas the fat-tailed gecko uses its tail. In times of plenty, this desert lizard stocks up on fat in its tail as a store of nutrients and energy for the lean times. After periods of scarcity, the tail has slimmed back down.

ABOVE:

Rain frog
Found in the semideserts of eastern and southern Africa, this amphibian is well named. It spends most of the year underground, protected in a bubble of slime. When the rains come, the frog emerges on the surface, feeding on insects and breeding vigorously.

RIGHT AND OPPOSITE:

South African springhare
Is it a kangaroo? Is it a rabbit? In fact, it is a large African rodent that has adopted a saltatorial, or hopping, locomotion to bound across the grasslands of southern and eastern Africa.

ALL PHOTOGRAPHS:
Aadvark
The first animal to appear in the dictionary, the name aardvark translates from the Afrikaans term 'earth pig'. The animal spends the day underground, and snuffles around by night using its nose and ears to find ants and termites. It uses long claws to dig into their mounds and nests, and then slurps them up with its long tongue.

Australasia

The smallest continent is also the one that has been most isolated from the rest of the world for longest, and as such it is home to a completely unique set of animals. Famously, Australia – a mostly arid land with large areas of a desert, dry scrub and woodlands – is home to marsupials, such as kangaroos, koalas and wombats. All are familiar, but nonetheless rather strange.

Marsupials are mammals in that they feed their young on milk and they have hairy bodies. However, they differ from the mammals that dominate the rest of the world since the females do not have a uterus able to hold a developing baby for more than a single oestrus (or menstrual cycle). As a result, a marsupial baby is born very early, when it is hairless, blind and wormlike, with just two front legs. The tiny baby, or joey, must haul itself a few centimetres to a place of safety – its mother's marsupium, which is a cosy pouch with teats inside. The joey completes its development there, going through all the growth stages that happen *in utero* in placental mammals. Despite this reproductive difference, marsupials have taken up life in all parts of Australia, and we shall see how they survive there in strange ways.

Australia has many other strange animals, including monotremes, which are mammals that lay eggs. Across the ocean, New Zealand is a land with few native mammals, being home instead to giant parrots, hefty grasshoppers and the flightless kiwi, among others.

OPPOSITE:
Emu
In addition to its strange-looking nest and distinctive green eggs, the emu is unusual because it is the male that broods the eggs and raises the chicks.

ALL PHOTOGRAPHS:
Land-based speedster
Standing proud as the second tallest bird in the world (reaching up to 1.9 m/6.2 ft), the emu is Australia's largest bird and fastest runner. It is a distant cousin of the ostrich, and it too lacks the sturdy breast muscles needed for flight, though the birds do flap their wings while running to help with balance. Their three-toed feet are built for running, with soft pads underneath and thick claws that are used to deliver a dangerous defensive kick. Female emus are bigger than the males, and they fight each other for mates.

Duck-billed platypus
Few animals are stranger than this aquatic hunter. The famed duck bill is actually a detector that picks up the electrical currents produced by freshwater crustaceans and other prey in dark, muddy water. Back on land, the strangeness continues. Instead of giving birth, the platypus lays small, leathery eggs from which its young hatch.

ALL PHOTOGRAPHS:
Archerfish
These sharp-shooting fish can
bring down an insect perched
on branches hanging some
3 m (9.8 ft) above with a jet of
water spat from the surface.

Dingo
This wild dog is one of the few non-marsupial mammals that lives naturally in Australia. However, it is descended from domestic dogs that were brought to Australia by human immigrants about 8,000 years ago. Once returned to the wild, the dog resumed a wolf-like lifestyle and now generally lives and hunts in packs. For the most part, it survives in balance with Australia's other animals, although it is likely that the thylacine, the marsupial tiger, became extinct on the mainland because of competition with the dingo.

ABOVE AND RIGHT:
Echidna
Also called a spiny anteater, the spikes covering these little creatures are thickened hair shafts. The echidna is related to the platypus. It too lay eggs, and the pointed snout is sensitive to electricity given out by insect prey.

OPPOSITE:
Kea
New Zealand is a land of birds, and the kea is a parrot from the mountains of the South Island. It has evolved to live as a spirited scavenger, grabbing food from tourists and feasting on the carcasses of sheep, and is thus more akin to a gull or crow than a macaw chattering in a forest tree.

Frilled lizard

What would you do if this fearsome-looking creature came at you, its head suddenly appearing to get larger and dominated by a big, gaping mouth? To be on the safe side, it's likely you'd run away. Indeed, this insect-eating, tree-living lizard from the Australian Outback uses this technique to see off threats as it races across open patches of ground.

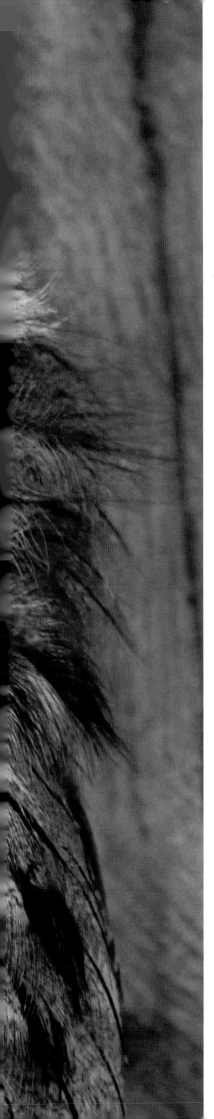

ALL PHOTOGRAPHS:
Frogmouth
These nocturnal Australian birds are relatives of the nightjar. They are named after their huge, gaping mouths, which they use for guzzling insects. By day, the compact birds sit stock still in a tree, so that the drab greys and browns of their fluffy plumage makes them look like small stumps on a branch.

ALL PHOTOGRAPHS:

Sydney funnel-web spider

Smaller than is often imagined – seldom more than 4 cm (1.6 in) long – this much-feared spider can deliver fatal bites with its gargantuan fangs (relative to its body size). The male spiders on a quest to find mates are the most dangerous because they cross paths with humans more frequently. Bites are nevertheless rare and there have been no lethal events since 1981, thanks to the development of an antivenom.

ABOVE:
Funnel web
The Sydney funnel-web is one of many types of spider that is named after the shape of its silken nest. Funnel-web spiders from outside of Australia are harmless to humans.

RIGHT:
Wētā
The wētā is a monstrous relative of the grasshopper that has evolved to eat seeds and shoots, taking the role filled by the mice in other parts of the world.

OVERLEAF:
Heavy insects
Wētās are flightless; they lack even vestigial wings. This is because they are far too heavy to get off the ground. The heaviest weighs in at 70 g (2.5 oz).

Honeypot ant
A worker ant always puts the needs of the colony before its own. These
ants from the arid Outback have specialized workers called repletes
that serve as a living food store, with abdomens that are swollen with a
sugary liquid. Hungry workers stroke the repletes' antennae, whereupon
they regurgitate some liquid for them.

ALL PHOTOGRAPHS:
Kākāpo
The kākāpo is the world's largest parrot, growing to 64 cm (25 in) long, not including the tail. It is too heavy and fat to fly and has only small wings. The bird, now extremely rare, lives on the forest floor, often clambering around inside bushes to find leaves, fruits and seeds to eat. The kākāpo also has the world's loudest bird call – the males make deep booming calls that can be heard 5 km (3.1 miles) away.

BOTH PHOTOGRAPHS:

Koala

Frequently referred to as a koala 'bear', this Australian icon is obviously a marsupial, and not related to true bears. The sluggish koala eats a diet composed almost exclusively of eucalyptus leaves. These are filled with pungent oils that turn the stomach of most herbivores, but the koala is immune to the toxins and slowly digests the food using a host of gut bacteria.

Peacock spider
This Australian jumping spider is named after is vibrant colouring. It does not set webbed traps for its prey, but instead makes great leaps many times its body length (which is only 5 mm/0.2 in). To hit the target, the spider has six eyes, four of which point forwards to pinpoint the exact position of prey.

ABOVE:

Peacock spider
Only the adult male of the species shows off the brightest colouring, taking the risk of attack to attract a mate. The colouring is even more vibrant when viewed under UV light. The females and juveniles are mostly brown.

RIGHT:

Laughing kookaburra
Named for its loud, repetitive call, this Australian hunting bird is a large relative of the kingfishers seen around the world. Instead of diving into water, the kookaburra jumps down from low branches to grab insect prey in dry forests.

ABOVE:
A mate for life
The laughing kookaburra is a
big bird, growing to about 45 cm
(18 in) long. It mates for life, and
builds its nest in a tree hollow.

RIGHT:
Kiwi
The namesake of all New
Zealanders, this medium-sized
flightless bird is a nocturnal
forager. It has nostrils on the tip
of its long beak and uses them to
sniff out grubs and worms in the
soil. It then plunges its beak into
the earth to grab its prey.

ALL PHOTOGRAPHS:
Red kangaroo
The largest wild land animal in Australia, the red kangaroo stands at about 1.5 m (4.9 ft) tall and weighs in at a maximum of 90 kg (198 lb). The kangaroo famously hops along on long, elastic back feet. The thick, 1.2 m (3.9 ft)-long tail helps balance out the body as the beast bounces along, and is used to provide a third point of support when the kangaroo is standing still. In line with all marsupials, the kangaroo gives birth to a very undeveloped baby, or joey, which then lives inside a pouch on the mother's belly to complete its development.

Sugar glider
It might look like a flying
squirrel but that is the power
of convergent evolution. This
nocturnal marsupial, which lives
in the treetops of Australia and
New Guinea, has a membrane of
skin running between its front and
back legs, which acts as a gliding
surface. This extends the distances
– up to 50 m (164 ft) – the little
creature can leap from tree to tree.

Thorny devil
The fleshy spines on this terrifying
desert lizard (although never fear,
it is only 20 cm/8 in long) have
two functions. First, they offer
an obvious defence, but they
also collect droplets of morning
dew, and this water trickles along
grooves between the spines all the
way to the mouth.

False head

The thorny devil carries a pair of bulbous spines on the back of its neck. This is to trick predators, who mistake the spines for the lizard's head and strike in a relatively harmless part of the body. The sharp prickles from the spines see off the attack and the delicate sense organs on the head are spared any damage.

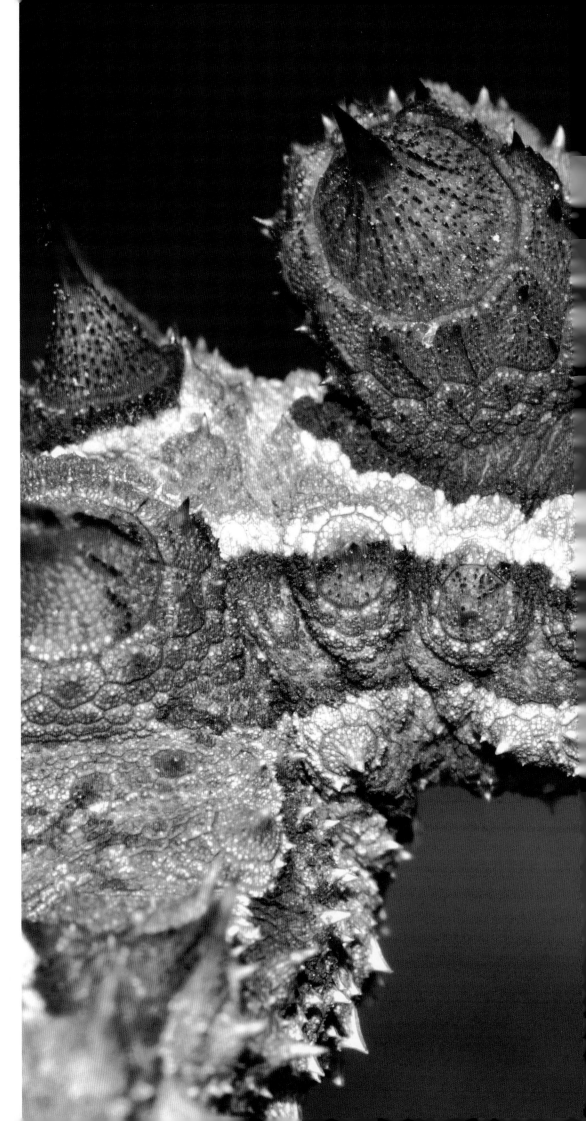

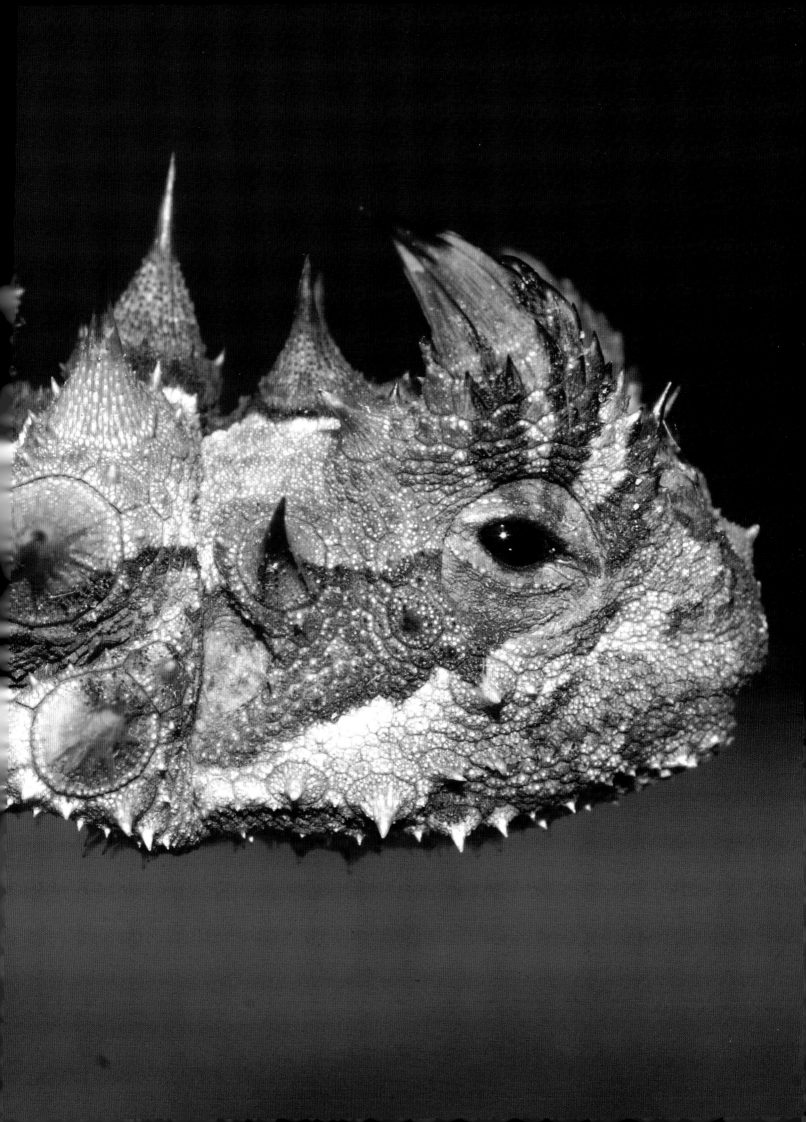

ALL PHOTOGRAPHS:
Tasmanian devil
Confined to Tasmania until recently, this chunky critter has been reintroduced in southern Australia. It is about 60 cm (24 in) long and 8 kg (17.6 lb) in weight, which makes it the biggest marsupial predator. Its sturdy frame and powerful jaw packs a punch, and a devil might try its luck against a small kangaroo. The nocturnal devil is so named because of the terrifying shrieks it emits in the darkness.

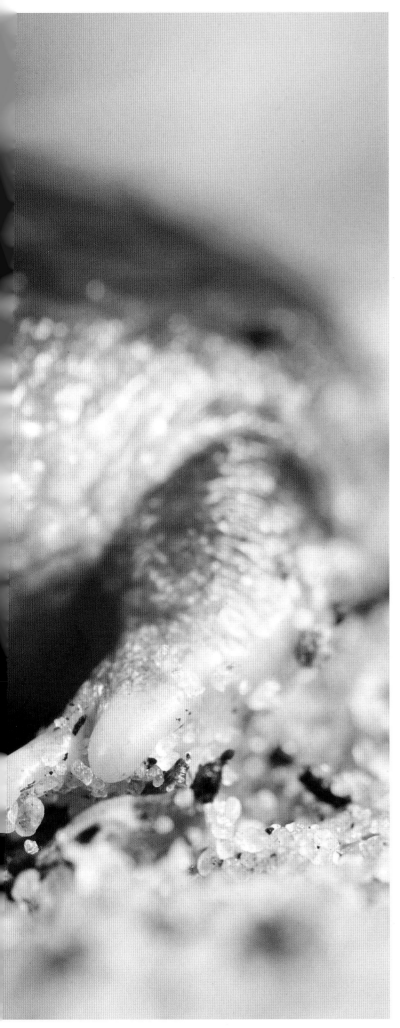

ALL PHOTOGRAPHS:

Turtle frog

Unusually, this frog from the dry forests of Western Australia does not bother with the tadpole stage; it hatches from the egg as a tiny frog. Its square shoulders and small head help with digging, which is fortunate, since this frog spends a lot of time hauling itself through the sand and dried mud of mounds built by termites, its primary food.

OVERLEAF:

Tuatara

This unique New Zealand creature looks like a lizard but is in fact the last surviving member of a group of reptiles that evolved around the same time as the dinosaurs – but saw less success. The tuatara breeds very slowly, with females laying one egg every four years.

Peaks on the back

The name tuatara comes from the Maori word for 'peaks on the back', a reference to the row of spikes along the spine. The 80 cm (32 in)-long tuatara is in grave peril of extinction because rats and other predators introduced to New Zealand destroy its eggs, which must incubate for more than a year. As a result, the tuatara only lives wild on a few rat-free islands.

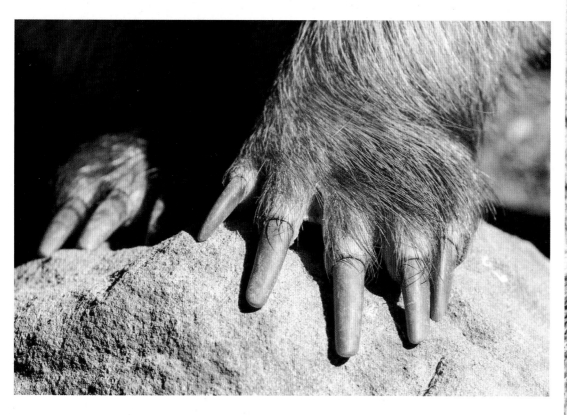

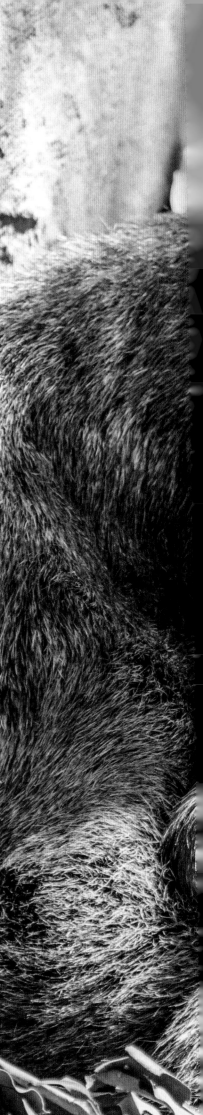

ALL PHOTOGRAPHS:

Wombat

These hefty burrowing grass-eaters have an odd claim to fame: they are the world's most dangerous marsupial. When threatened, they turn tail and present a rock-hard rear that is impervious to bites. Next, they reverse charge, and a bash from the butt can crush a foe's skull – in theory. Wombats also use their rumps to knock down mating rivals and curious humans who come too close – and then bash them repeatedly.

In addition, wombats have a powerful bite and a sturdy set of claws for digging burrows, which are also a threat to life and limb, although there are no reports of fatalities. They generally produce one joey at a time. And a final strangeness: wombats do cube-shaped droppings!

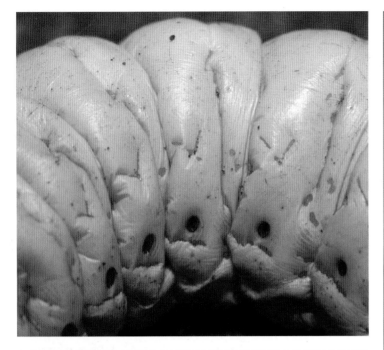

ALL PHOTOGRAPHS:
Witchetty grub
Famed as an example of 'bush tucker', or food sourced from the seemingly barren Outback, this grub is actually a fat moth caterpillar. Several tasty species are eaten but the most common is the cossid moth. The grub lives underground, feeding on the roots of the witchetty bush, a type of acacia.

North America

This continent contains a large swathe of Arctic tundra and cold, boreal forest of pine and other conifers. There are two big mountain ranges, both running north to south, with very different animals living in them. In between, there are vast prairies and plains. In the south, North America extends through Mexico all the way the Panama, and so has tropical deserts and rainforests. North and South America have only relatively recently joined together, after spending millions of years apart. In fact, the animal community of North America has more in common with that of Eurasia. The wolverine, the moose, the wolf, the brown bear; these big mammals are found across the boreal habitats of the Northern Hemisphere. Meanwhile, there is not much mixing between the animal populations north and south. The Isthmus of Panama, still a place of dense jungles and rugged hills, has been an effective barrier to all but the hardiest creatures.

Nevertheless, North America has some strange residents. One such noteworthy species is the bullfrog, a rowdy member of the community that makes its presence felt with its loud calls. America has its fair share of big critters, too, from the beaver, which is a rodent that cuts down trees; a peccary, which is a bellicose relative to the wild boar; and the alligator snapping turtle, which could cut off your finger. And that does not even begin to express the strangeness of the star-nosed mole, Gila monster and hellbender.

OPPOSITE:
American bullfrog
This mighty frog is named for the deep bellow used to attract females. Some males sit quietly beside the loudest and deepest-voiced males and intercept any interested females.

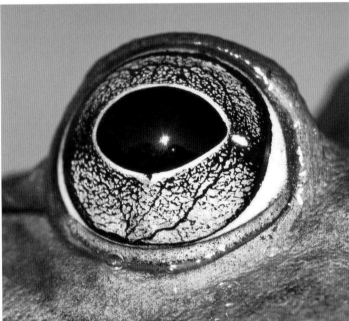

ALL PHOTOGRAPHS THIS PAGE:

Down in one

Big and noisy, the bullfrog is an all-American amphibian. It is supremely adapted to life in swamps and rivers – anywhere that is wet enough. It can grow to 15 cm (6 in) long, and is much bigger when its limbs are outstretched. It will eat whatever animal it can swallow. Food is swallowed whole, the big eyes on top of the bullfrog's head being pulled down to give meals an extra push down the throat.

RIGHT:

Beaver

Few animals are as iconic as this semi-aquatic rodent. It is famed for felling trees with its powerful gnawing teeth, and using the logs to dam rivers. The reason for doing so is to create a lush wetland upstream, where the beaver can feed on grasses. In winter, it survives on wood left to soak in water. Beaver dams are a nuisance in intensively managed landscapes, but if they are given space, landowners are beginning to realize their benefits in controlling flooding and boosting biodiversity.

OVERLEAF:

American white pelican

With a wingspan of nearly 3 m (9.8 ft) and weighing in at 13 kg (28.7 lb), this is one of the biggest flying birds in the world. It makes short flights over water, searching for fish. It then lands on the surface and scoops up the food in its sac-like beak. The lower part of the beak is a flexible bag of skin. The bird drains the water from the bag, trapping the fish inside – which is then swallowed whole.

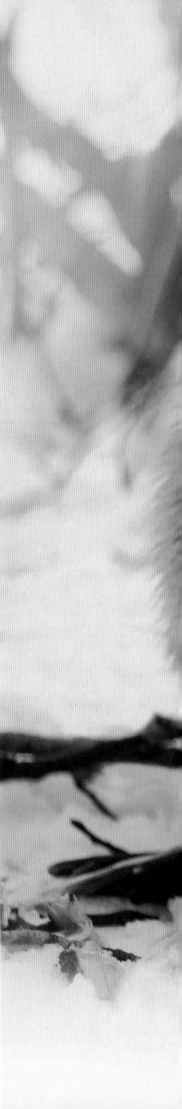

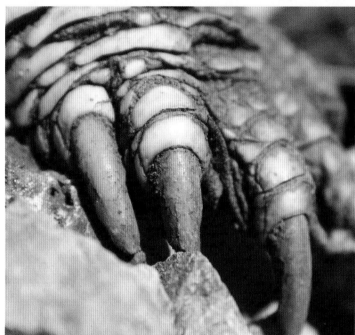

ALL PHOTOGRAPHS:
Alligator snapping turtle
This monstrous river turtle is the
biggest freshwater turtle in North
America, and the most feared. The
beak may be toothless but it is
sharp enough to slice off a finger
with a single snap. Thankfully, the
snapping turtle is mostly found at
the bottom of the rivers and lakes
in the southeast of the United
States. Down there, it uses a bright
worm-shaped flash of red on its
tongue to lure in fish, which are
gobbled up and never seen again.

ABOVE AND RIGHT:

Collared peccary

They may look like wild boars but these squat, hoofed creatures from the arid scrublands of Texas and Mexico are in fact distant cousins to the pigs and wild hogs. They have the same blunt snout for sniffing out food in leaf litter or buried in the mud. Wild peccaries are often in conflict and are also known as javelinas because they frequently show off their spiked canine teeth.

OPPOSITE:

Blue-footed booby

This startling seabird is well named for its dazzling feet. The second part of its name comes from the Spanish for 'stupid person'. The Pacific shore birds, which live in the Gulf of California, lack fear of humans and so would land on ships, enabling sailors to simply pick them up. Their blue feet are a sign of good health and are most important during elaborate courtship rituals.

LEFT:
Star-nosed mole
The fingered snout of this small burrowing animal is a touch and electrical sensor, not a smelling organ. It is covered with 25,000 receptors in total, which pick up the electricity given out by the muscles and nerves of worms and other prey in the soil.

ABOVE TOP:
Hellbender
This is the largest amphibian in North America. The giant salamander spends its days in fast-flowing mountain streams, preying on crayfish and other small water animals. The cold, clear water is full of oxygen, so the big hellbender can absorb the oxygen it needs directly through its wrinkled skin.

ABOVE BOTTOM:
Stinkpot
Also called the common musk turtle, this freshwater reptile is named after the way it releases a foul-smelling liquid from glands around the edge of the shell. Few predators proceed with an attack after encountering this.

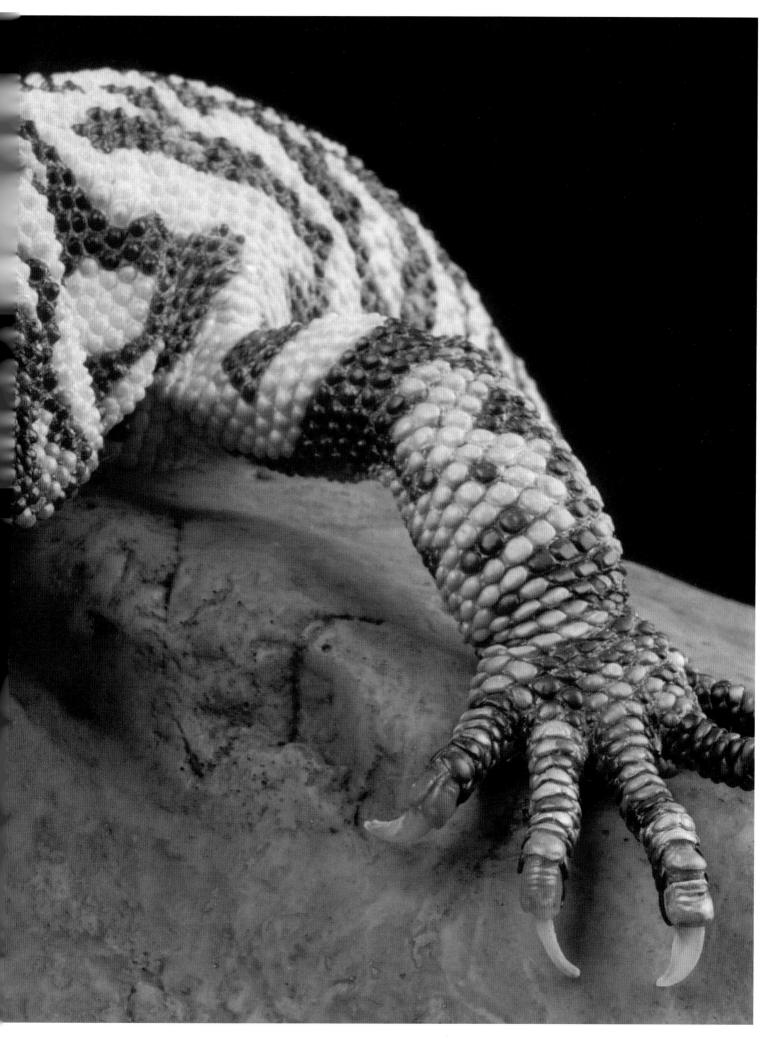

PREVIOUS PAGES:
Gila monster
Growing to more than 50 cm (20 in) long, this slow-moving, chunky reptile is the one of a very few venomous lizards in North America. (The others are the related beaded lizards from Mexico.) The Gila monster lumbers through the desert borderlands eating mice and small birds. Its venom, in the saliva, is mostly harmless to humans.

ALL PHOTOGRAPHS:
Virginia opossum
This strange-looking climbing mammal is a marsupial, which raises its young in a marsupium, or pouch, on the belly. Despite what many might think, marsupials did not arise in Australia. Rather, they are thought to have evolved in North America but died out there after spreading to South America and on to Australia via Antarctica (these continents were all connected back then, and much warmer). The Virginia opossum was one of a very few species that made it back into North America and it proved very successful there. It is the northernmost marsupial, found all the way up to Canada.

ALL PHOTOGRAPHS:

Manatee

Manatees are sea cows that live in the tropical Atlantic. The West Indian species lives in the mangrove swamps along the Gulf of Mexico, Florida and the Caribbean. Each manatee is a big beast, weighing 0.5 tonnes (0.55 tons), and powerfully odorous thanks to its diet of seagrasses that need a lot of digestion and produce a lot of gas.

ALL PHOTOGRAPHS:

Monarch butterfly

This large American butterfly is famed for making an epic migration from the meadows and forests of North America as far north as the Great Lakes, to wintering grounds in Mexico and California. There, it perches in trees, where it avoids the frost. Birds know not to eat them – the bright orange colours are a signal that the insect does not taste very nice. This is because as a caterpillar, the monarch feasts on milkweed, which has a toxic sap. These toxins are stored in the body and passed on to the adult as it emerges from the chrysalis.

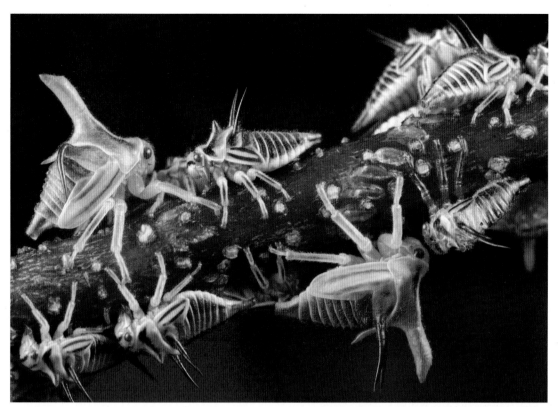

OPPOSITE AND LEFT:
Thorn bug
This sap-sucking insect belongs to a group called the treehoppers. It sits on a twig and jabs it pointed mouthpart into plants. The insect has to sit still as it drinks the low-quality food. To defend against attack, its thorax does a very good job of looking like a sturdy thorn.

BELOW BOTH PHOTOGRAPHS:
Alligator gar
This long fish from the Mississippi Basin is a so-called 'living fossil'. It evolved at least 100 million years ago and has a body system that is very different to the ones used by the great majority of fish today. It grows to 1.8 m (5.9 ft) long and weighs up to 50 kg (110 lb). It earns its name from the wide, square jaw, which holds many small but sharp teeth.

Wolverine
This is the largest weasel in the world, growing to about 1 m (3.3 ft) long. The wolverine is a hunter, and in summer it preys on small rodents and rabbits. However, it is in winter that the wolverine comes into its own. The bears in the cold, northern forests it calls home are hibernating at this time of year, so the wolverine is one of the toughest animals around. Thanks to its wide feet, it is able to cross deep snow and take on big animals such as deer and bison that have become stuck.

PREVIOUS PAGE:
Red wolf
This rare species of wild dog is midway between a grey wolf and a coyote in terms of size. It almost became extinct in the wild thanks to persecution from farmers in the eastern United States. In the late 1980s, captive-bred red wolves were released into protected areas in North Carolina. However, its future is not assured as wild red wolves breed with coyotes, creating unwanted hybrid offspring.

RIGHT ALL PHOTOGRAPHS:
White-nosed coati
This relative of the raccoon is able to survive in a wide range of habitats from the deserts of the US southwest all the way through Central America to the tropical forests of Colombia. It is an omnivore that searches high and low for something to eat.

OPPOSITE:
Spirit bear
It might not look like it, but this is a subspecies of the American black bear. The pale, ghost-like spirit bears live in a patch of coastal rainforest and islands in British Columbia. It is not an albino bear but instead lacks the genes for growing dark fur. Nevertheless, it blends in well enough in a dappled glade.

Rubber boa

This strange desert snake is named after its smooth skin made from tiny scales. The docile, nocturnal snake ties itself into a knot when threatened, leaving its blunt tail exposed but hiding the head, in the hope that a predator will confuse the two.

Central & South America

This is the most biodiverse part of the planet. About 60 per cent of the land plants and animals on Earth live in this region, mostly in the dense tropical forests that cover large areas. One forest resident is the emperor tamarin, which has a moustache to rival any militarist ruler. The little monkey was specifically named because it looks like a tiny version of Kaiser Wilhelm II, the last emperor of Germany. Tamarins and their equally diminutive cousins the marmosets are examples of New World monkeys, which live only in Central and South America. They differ from the Old World monkeys of Africa and Asia by having wider, flatter noses. Some also have prehensile tails that work like a fifth limb.

As well as monkeys, the rainforest is packed with life, often strange, and far too numerous to fit into one book. There are hundreds of species to be found in just one tree, making it a unique wildlife community that will be quite distinct from that found in another tree only a short walk away in the forest.

Away from the forests, South America has the steep peaks of the Andes, the world's longest mountain range. Its foothills in the north look over the humid Caribbean Sea, while in the south, they slope down to the shores of the icy Southern Ocean. Strangely, the Andes are home to camels, or at least humpless close relations. Meanwhile, the continent's largest predatory mammal might also be nearby – eating some fruit.

OPPOSITE:
Emperor tamarin
This little monkey lives in the heart of the Amazon, far from the Atlantic coast, in the region of the forest below the eastern slopes of the Andes.

Axolotl

This unique amphibian is named
after the Aztec god of fire and
lightning. During Aztec times
the axolotl lived wild in the lakes
and waterways of Tenochtitlan,
the old imperial capital. Today,
that is the site of Mexico city, and
the axolotl's wetland habitat has
been considerably shrunk. The
amphibian spends all of its life
in water, unlike almost all other
amphibians, which transform from
a young aquatic form with gills
into an air-breathing adult.

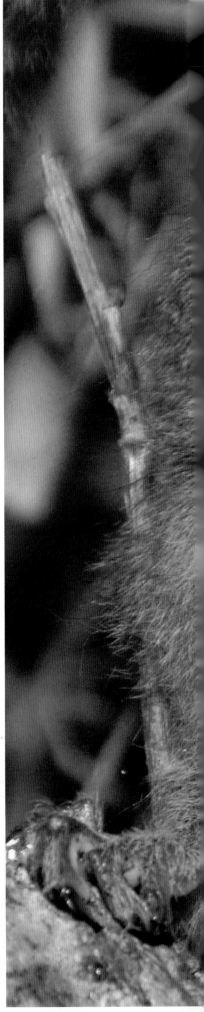

ABOVE AND RIGHT:

Horned frog

These big frogs from the forests of
South America are named for the
spike-like 'eyebrows'. They also
have the nickname of the Pacman
frog because they have a mouth so
big they can consume a meal that
is bigger than they are. They eat
anything from crickets to rats –
and have even been known to eat
their mates.

FAR RIGHT:

Pygmy marmoset

This is the smallest monkey species
of all. Even the adults weigh a
mere 100 g (3.5 oz) and grow
to 13 cm (5.1 in) long. They are
small enough to perch on thick
grass stalks, but they are mostly
found in the dense understory of
Amazon rainforests, where they eat
the sweet gums and resins exuded
from trees.

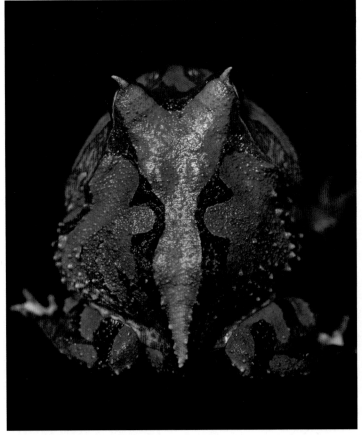

Hoatzin

This strange Amazonian bird defies simple classification and has no close relatives. Experts now think the hoatzin, or 'stinky turkey' as the locals might call it, is a distant cousin of wading birds. The species lives close to water, mostly eating the leaves in trees that grow above swamps. It has two claws in the middle of its wings – a very primitive feature of birds – which are used to grip branches as the bird clambers around inside a tree.

OPPOSITE:
Elephant beetle
The trunk-like horn that earns this forest insect its name grows from the face of the males only. It is used as a symbol of status during the battle for mates. The bigger horn wins conflicts, and when it is too close to call, the males will use their horn to push a rival off the branch. Some of these beetles can grow to 15 cm (6 in).

LEFT AND BELOW:
Capybara
Known by locals as a water pig, this is actually the world's largest rodent. It is a giant relative of the guinea pig that grows to 130 cm (51 in) long and can weigh as much as 60 kg (132 lb). Capybara herds graze in lush meadows beside rivers, and the animals dash into the shallows when they feel threatened.

ABOVE:
Vicuña
This is the wild relative of the alpaca, and shares South America's high and dry habitats with the guanaco, which is the wild relative of the llama. The vicuña, a type of humpless camel, lives on the high slopes of the Andes. It grows a thick fleece of wool to keep out the cold air.

RIGHT:
Three-toed sloth
There are four species of sloth with three claws on the forelegs. They live across the forested regions of South and Central America. Famously slow, sloths eat large quantities of leaves and hang about digesting much of the time. They sleep, mate and give birth upside down.

ALL PHOTOGRAPHS:
Marine iguana
The Galápagos Islands, located about 1,000 km (621 miles) west of the Ecuadorian mainland, are home to many strange animals. The marine iguana is one of the most striking. It is the only lizard species in the world that sources its food from the sea. The 80 cm (32 in)-long lizard dives down several metres to graze on seaweeds. It drinks seawater in the process and snorts out the unwanted salt through the nose, leaving a white crust on its face.

OVERLEAF LEFT:
Piranha
The piranha's sharp teeth represent a serious weapon, delivering the strongest bite of any fish other than sharks. Its reputation for frenzied attacks is misplaced, although schools can causes significant injuries if they are trapped in small pools and have no means of escape.

OVERLEAF RIGHT:
Jaguarundi
This wild cat is about twice the size of a house cat. It is named with a term from the native language of what is now Paraguay (and has the same linguistic root as jaguar, a much bigger American cat). It lives across the continent, hunting by day in forests, grasslands and deserts.

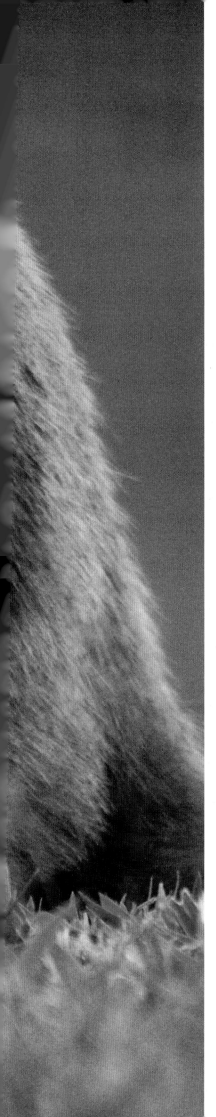

LEFT:
Southern tamandua
This is a small relative of the better-known giant anteater. It sleeps in a tree hollow by day and then by night climbs into the treetops to eat fruits and honey and slurp up the ants and termites that dash around the branches. Down on the ground, it digs into nests to find more insect prey.

ABOVE TOP:
Pink fairy armadillo
The smallest species of armadillo, this cute-looking creature is only about 10 cm (4 in) long. It lives in the dry grasslands of Argentina. It has reduced armour and a torpedo-shaped body because it spends much of its time burrowing underground, eating whatever invertebrates it finds.

ABOVE BOTTOM:
Spectacled bear
So named because of the large dark rings around its eyes, this is the largest hunter in South America. However, despite that title, the bear, which patrols the damp forests of the Andes mountains, eats a lot more fruit and other plant food than freshly killed prey.

ABOVE:

Pink river dolphin

Also called the boto or Amazon river dolphin, this lives all over the Amazon and Orinoco river basins. It has a more flexible body than ocean dolphins so it can hunt for fish among the trunks and roots of flooded forests. The dolphin is born grey but becomes pinker as its skin rubs against objects.

RIGHT:

Roseate spoonbill

The splendid pink feathers of this spoonbill are coloured by chemicals in the shrimps and other foods that it sifts from rivers, lakes and shallow coastal waters. The nostrils are positioned high up the bill, so the bird can keep breathing as it sweeps its mouth through the water collecting food.

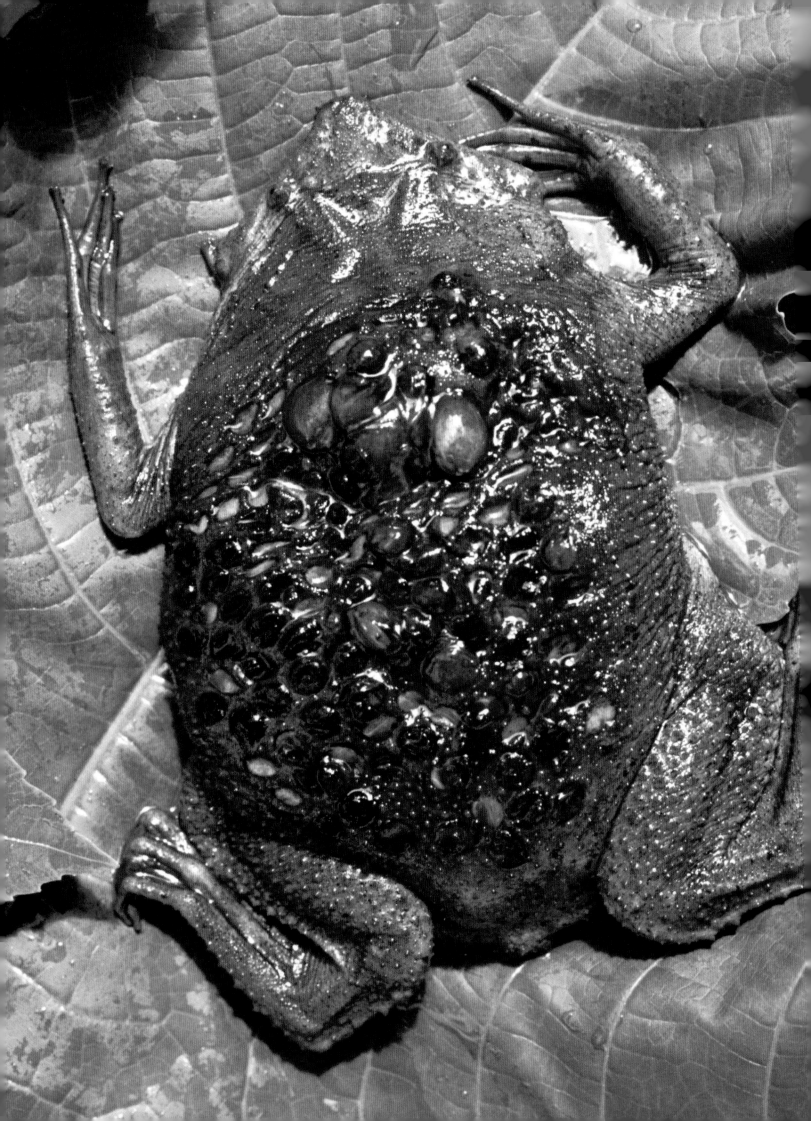

ALL PHOTOGRAPHS:
Surinam toad
This rainforest frog spends it whole life in water. It has a very flattened body and lies in the mud on the bottom of forest rivers, looking like a fallen leaf as it waits to ambush small fish, shrimps or worms. During mating, the male shoves the sticky fertilized eggs on to the female's back. The skin grows around them, and the eggs develop inside fleshy capsules.

179

ABOVE AND RIGHT:

Vampire bat

It may be a surprise to hear that it is very strange for bats to drink blood, but that is exactly how these long-fanged flyers get their food. Vampire bats rarely target humans, preferring larger beasts such as horses and cattle. They attack sleeping victims, making a small bite on some warm skin and licking up the blood that flows.

OPPOSITE:

Red howler monkey

At dawn, these big, leaf-eating monkeys stand up in their nests at the tops of the tallest forest trees and give out loud howls. The chorus travels some 5 km (3.1 miles) into the forest and reinforces territorial claims.

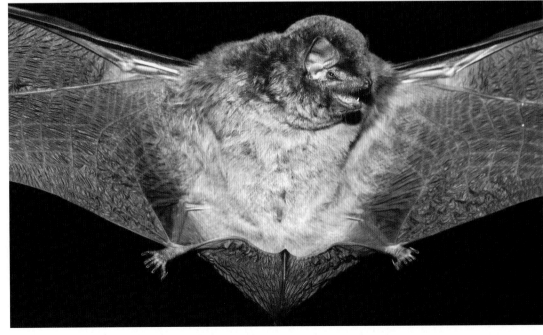

ALL PHOTOGRAPHS:
Red-lipped batfish
The name needs no explanation.
This species lives on the seabed
along the Pacific coast. It seldom
swims, but instead walks on the
sea floor using its stiffened fins. It
gobbles up small fish and shrimps
with its downturned mouth.

Europe

Europe is the most damaged continent on Earth. The countryside scenes from the Scottish glens to the rolling hills of Tuscany and pine forests of Germany are all unnatural habitats that have been created and managed by human activities. Beautiful they certainly are, but that beauty has been bought at the expense of biodiversity.

The natural habitats of Europe, certainly in the north and west, would be wetlands, deciduous forests and heathlands. The great majority of those habitats are now lost, and the native animals with them. The only truly wild places are locations unsuitable for human settlements, such the high alpine meadows where the Alpine ibex roams Europe's main mountain range. It is sure-footed enough to clamber around the steep rocky slopes that are beyond the reach of all but the hardiest human climbers.

In the east of the continent, significant fragments of ancient forest remain and these are home to the wisent, the largest wild land animal in Europe. In the rivers, there is something even bigger – the beluga sturgeon – although that is now very rare and seldom seen at full size. In the south, closer to the Mediterranean, the habitat is a mosaic of woodlands and shrubs. If you are lucky, you might see some strange lizards, such as a chameleon, or amphibians like the sharp-ribbed newt.

OPPOSITE:
Alpine ibex
The ibex has a wide gap between its hooves that widens as weight is applied to form a pincer-like grip on the rough ground.

ABOVE AND RIGHT:
Iberian ribbed newt
This is Europe's largest newt species. It grows to around 30 cm (12 in) long. The strangest thing about it becomes apparent when it is picked up. The pointed tips of the ribs push through the skin on the flanks, jabbing the attacker sufficiently for it to let go.

OPPOSITE ALL PHOTOGRAPHS:
Beluga sturgeon
The name means 'white' sturgeon in Russian, which refers to the pale belly. This species lives mostly in the river systems that feed the Caspian and Black seas. At a weight of 1.2 tonnes (1.3 tons) and a length of 6 m (19.7 ft), this species is the third largest type of bony fish. Today, it is hunted perilously close to extinction for its eggs, which are served as caviar.

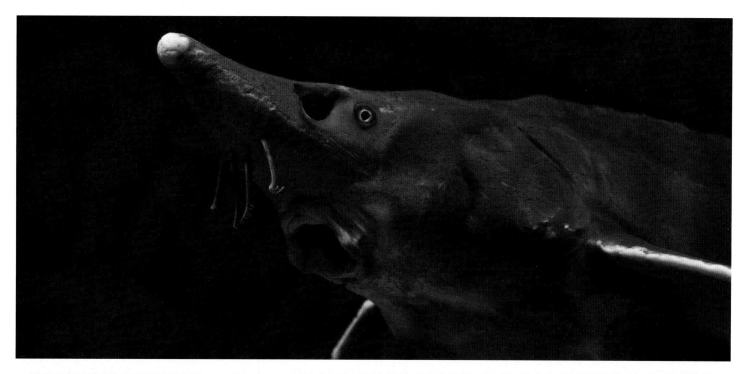

Common chameleon
This is the only chameleon species to live in Europe. It clings on in patches of forest along the southern coast and islands of the Mediterranean. Chameleons are obviously famed for their ability to change colour, although this is much more limited than in the popular imagination. Another strange feature is that the eyes move independently, searching in all directions for insect prey. It then splats them with a strike of its long tongue.

ABOVE AND RIGHT:

Common cuckoo

Arriving from Africa in spring, Eurasian cuckoos sound off their distinctive call to find a mate. The female then makes the most of her passing resemblance to a sparrow hawk to scare off warblers or other songbirds from their nests. Next, she lays a single egg among the hosts', and leaves. The interloper hatches first and shoves out all the other eggs. The tricked parents will feed their guest even as it grows much bigger than them.

OPPOSITE:

Badger

This chunky black-and-white beast is the toughest predator around in many parts of Europe, now that bears, wolves and lynxes are all but gone. It is no larger than a spaniel but potentially much fiercer.

ALL PHOTOGRAPHS:

Death's-head hawkmoth

This fast-flying, delta-winged moth migrates into Europe from Africa in summer. It is famed for the skull-shaped pattern on its thorax, which has led people to assume that the insect brings bad luck. It is certainly a bad omen for honeybees, because the yellow and black stripes on the abdomen are a rough disguise that enables it to invade nests. The moth also mimics the smell of the bees as it raids the supplies of honey and nectar. If spotted, the moth gives out a squeak, which is thought to sound like the piping noises issued by the queen bee as commands. This offers some respite, and the moth's thick skin protects it from stings as it makes its escape.

ALL PHOTOGRAPHS:
Great diving beetle
This big beetle hunts among the pondweed and other plants that grow in slow-flowing freshwater. The hairs on is long back legs make them work better as oars for paddling through the water. The beetle spends its larval period in water, and then metamorphoses on land into the boat-shaped adult form – which then promptly dives back into the water.

OPPOSITE:
Wisent
Also called the European bison, this is the largest wild land animal in Europe. It is a close relative of the American bison (or buffalo), although it is slightly smaller and less shaggy, plus it is a beast of the forest rather than the plains its American cousin prefers.

ABOVE AND LEFT:
Slow worm
This slithery fellow is indeed slow, but is neither a worm nor a snake. Instead, it is a legless lizard, the giveaway being that it has eyelids and so can blink – like a lizard but unlike a snake. Slow worms can be seen sunbathing but spend most of their time in warm, damp thickets, hunting for insects.

ALL PHOTOGRAPHS:
Atlantic puffin
After spending the winter out at sea, these distinctive sea birds congregate at breeding grounds in spring. The mature birds arrive with a brightly coloured bill to act as a sign of fertility and dominance. They nest in deep burrows in muddy cliffs, with pairs returning to the same nest year after year. Puffins eat nothing but fish, which they collect during short dives. They are able to collect several fish at once, holding them against the roofs of their mouths with their tongues as they snatch additional ones.

Wels catfish
This monstrous catfish lurks in the muddy depths of European rivers and lakes, and seldom makes an appearance at the surface. It grows to 3 m (9.8 ft) long and its name is derived from the German for 'whale'. The wels is a bottom feeder, slurping up worms and fish, which it finds by touch and smell. It also eats ducks, frogs and almost anything else that takes to the water.

Oceans

The oceans cover 70 per cent of the Earth's surface and make up about 99 per cent of all the space in the biosphere. However, only about 1 per cent of the planet's total biomass – that is, the weight of plants, animals and everything else – is found in the oceans.

The great majority of ocean life lives within 200 m (656 ft) of the surface, where it is light enough each day for plants and other photosynthetic organisms to survive. Below that, animals are the only large life forms and survive by feeding on each other and whatever falls from above.

This is a strange way to live and many marine animals are strange indeed. For example, the anglerfish, sometimes referred to by the more appetizing name of monkfish, is a hunter built for life on the seafloor or in deep, dark waters. It is so named because many of them attract smaller fish towards them with a lure that glows in the dark and is located on a spine above the mouth. It is a lonely life as an anglerfish, and the chances of meeting a mate are low, so a male takes no chances. When he find a female, he latches on to her flank and connects to her blood supply. Indeed, males degenerate into little more than a parasitic set of testes that produces sperm when the mate needs it.

If that were not strange enough, then read on to find out about a megamouth shark, a dumbo octopus and a crab that grows its own food.

OPPOSITE:
Anglerfish
This anglerfish off the coast of Bali, Indonesia, has some excellent camouflaging that makes it look like a rock covered in seaweed.

LEFT:

Christmas tree worm

Is it a seaweed? Is it an anemone? The clue is of course in the name, and it is in fact a worm, which grows on coral reefs around the world. The feathery tree-shaped appendages are used to collect food and oxygen from the water.

ABOVE TOP AND BOTTOM:

Dumbo octopus

Named after the big-eared flying elephant from the Disney movie, this deep-sea umbrella octopus searches the dark seabed for crustaceans and other prey. The ear-like fins are used for swimming in open water.

LEFT:
Giant isopod
This is a deep-sea crustacean that
has many features in common
with its terrestrial cousin, the
woodlouse. However, growing to
15 cm (6 in) long, it is truly
giant. The isopod lives on the sea floor,
scavenging for the remains of
animals such as whales that have
fallen from above.

ABOVE TOP AND BOTTOM:
Pacific hagfish
Primitive tubular fish like this
have been living on the sea floor
for hundreds of millions of years.
They are chiefly scavengers.
Hagfish have no jaw, but instead
have a spiral of teeth that they
twist into corpses to drill out a
cylinder of flesh.

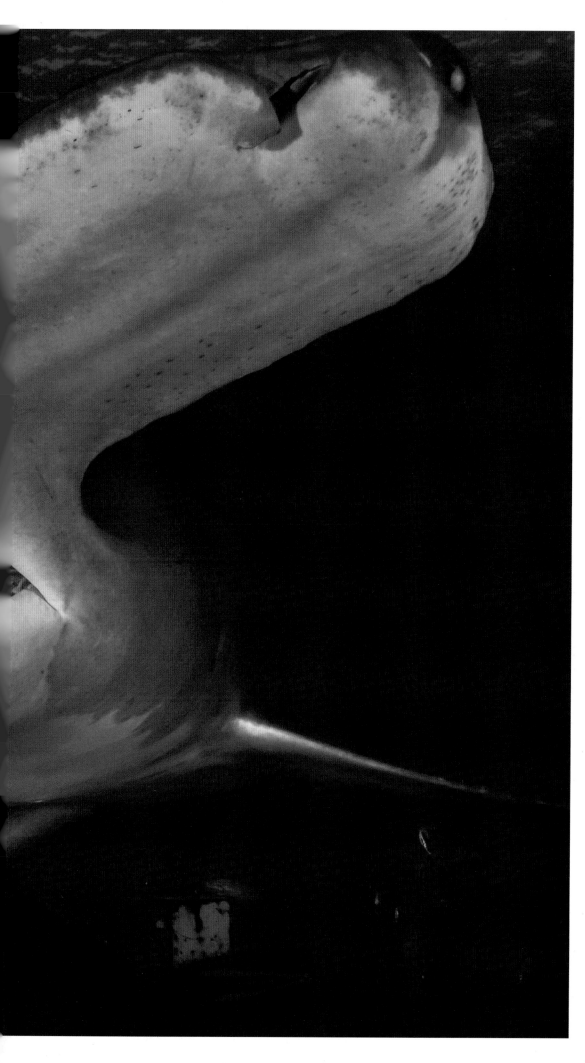

Hammerhead shark

One of the strangest hunters in the sea, these sharks are well named. The eyes and nostrils are widely spaced by a wing-shaped head. This set-up has multiple advantages. The wing shape helps create lift as the shark swims. The nostrils are far apart and that helps with detecting the direction of smells, with odours arriving on one side first. Finally, the underside of the wide head is covered in electrical receptors that sweep from side to side picking up signs of life in the water.

Coral
A well-known form of sea life, corals are a wide range of jellyfish-like animals that grow in vast, colourful colonies.

Megamouth shark
As the third largest shark in the sea, it is somewhat surprising that this filter feeder was only discovered in 1976. It patrols the twilight zone in the ocean and seldom comes to the surface.

Kiwa hirsuta
This strange crustacean lives around hydrothermal vents in the deep ocean, where the water is rich with nutrients. It eats the bacteria that thrive in these challenging conditions, and cultivates them in mats on its hairy pincers.

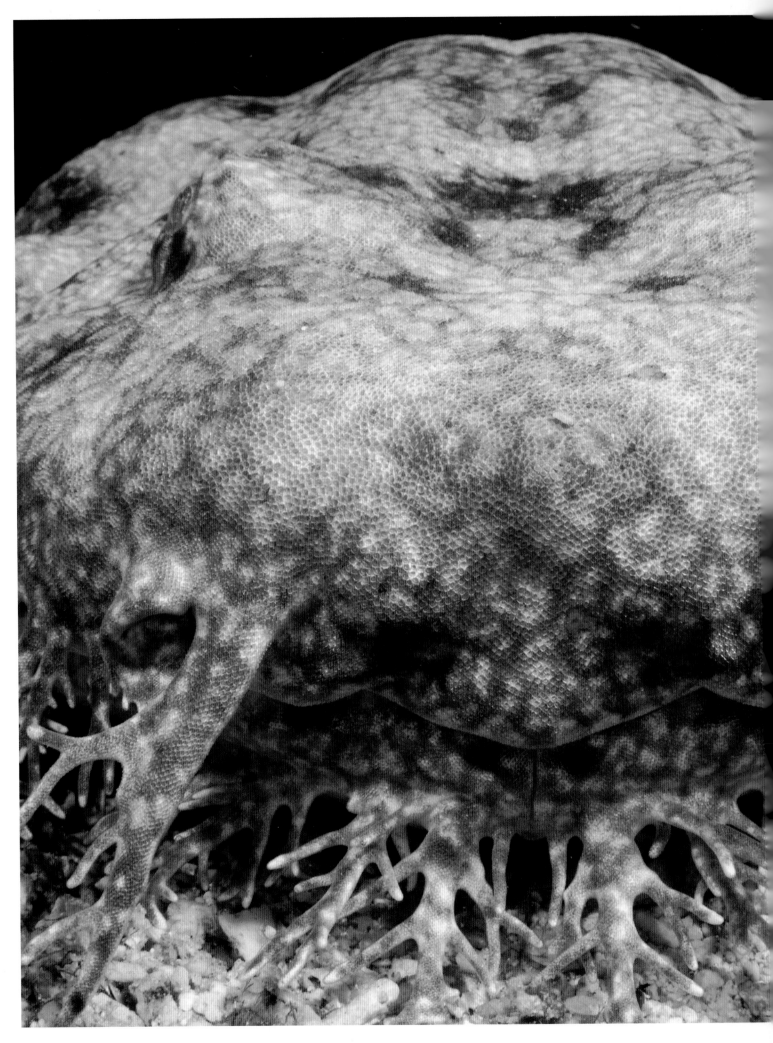

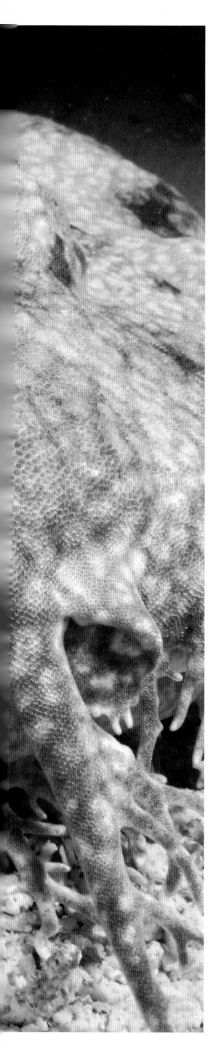

ALL PHOTOGRAPHS:

Wobbegong

This carpet shark (named for the bold repeating patterns) lives on the seabed of shallow coastal seas in the Indian and Pacific oceans. The name comes from an Australian Aboriginal language and means 'shaggy beard'. These whiskery lobes help break up the ambush hunter's body shape.

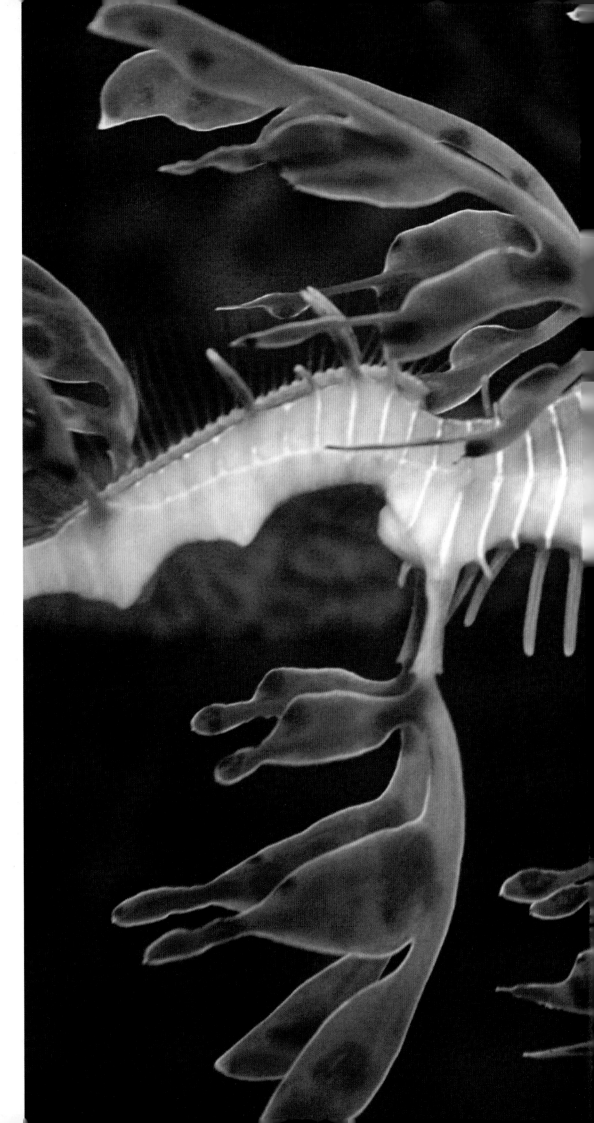

Leafy seadragon
This relative of the seahorses lives along the southern coast of Australia. Its fins and appendages resemble seaweeds and it lingers in weedy spots sucking up microscopic foods through its tubular snout. This way of life is shared by seahorses. All are at great risk from pollution and habitat destruction.

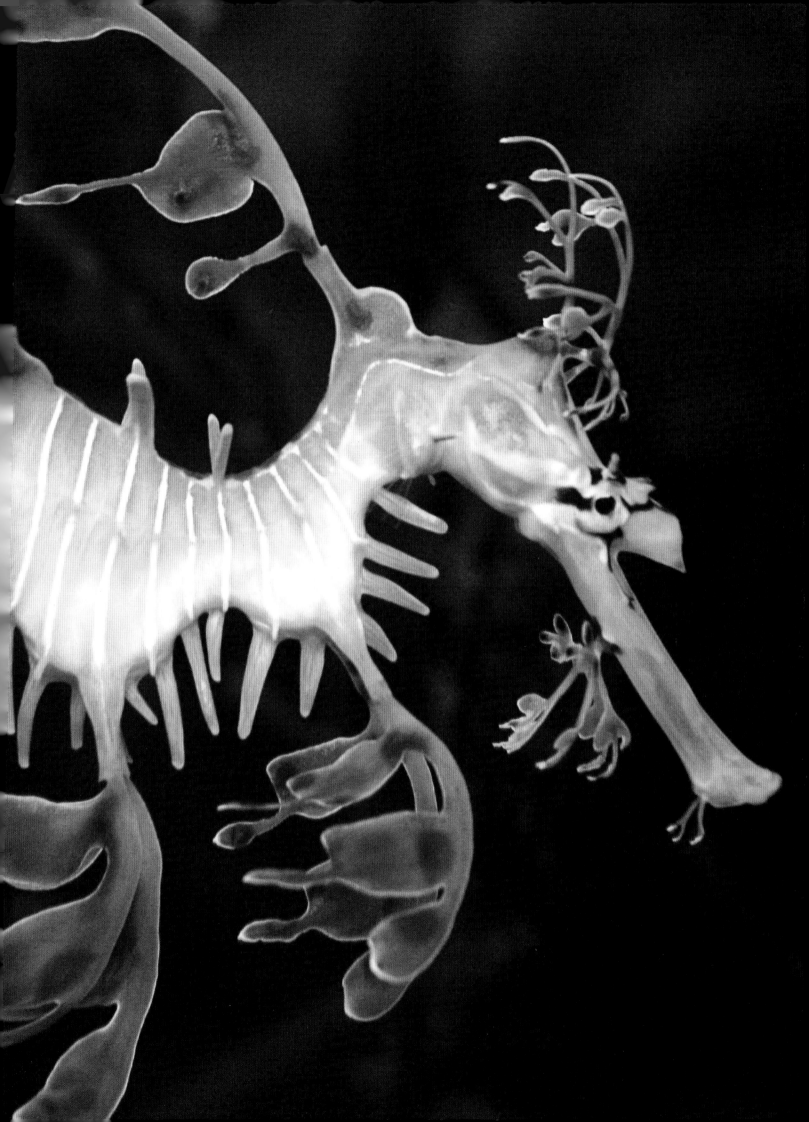

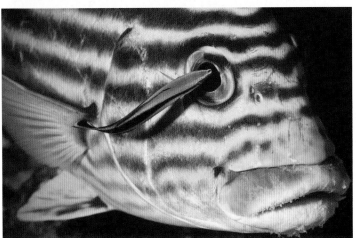

ABOVE ALL PHOTOGRAPHS:

Cleaner wrasse

These helpful little fish get their food supply from the bodies of other sea creatures. As their name suggests, they use their small pointed mouths to pluck off mites and other parasites as well as general organic gunk from larger creatures. Their hosts tolerate them and resist the urge to gobble up the little cleaner.

RIGHT:

Sea anemone

This is a sedentary relative of the jellyfish. It spends its life the other way up, with its tentacles pointing up and the body glued to a rock on the seabed. The tentacles are covered in poisoned stinger cells that jab into animals that brush past. The victim is then hauled into the central mouth.

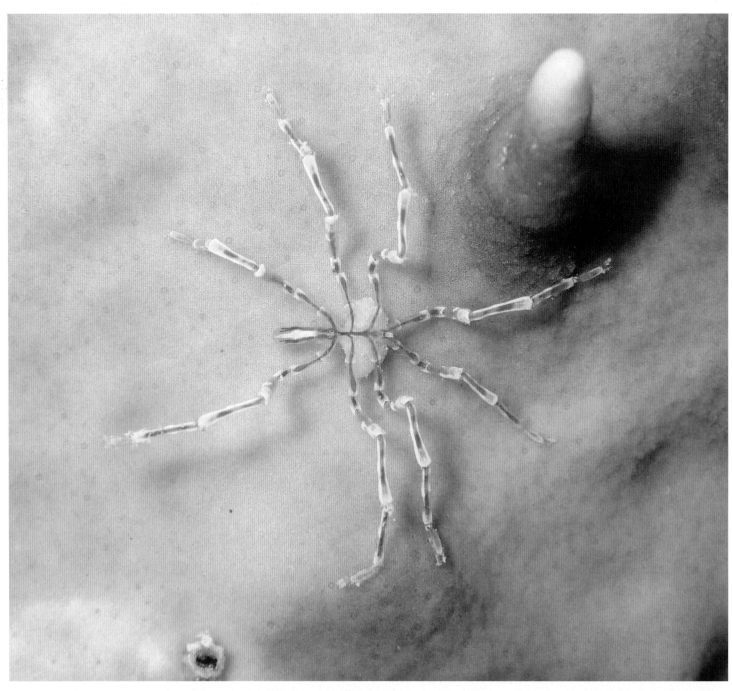

OPPOSITE TOP:
Sea spider
Spider by name but not by nature, this is an unusual distant relative of the arachnids that lives on the seabed, foraging for animal foods. They tend to be very small, perhaps only a few millimetres wide, but some grow to 70 cm (28 in) across.

OPPOSITE BOTTOM:
Narwhal
The unicorn of the sea, the male of this small toothed whale has a single straight, spiralled tusk that is in fact an enlarged front tooth. The length of the tusk is a sign of dominance, and it may also have sensory qualities. The narwhal is an Arctic hunter that sucks in fish and squid to its otherwise toothless mouth.

ALL PHOTOGRAPHS THIS PAGE:
Nudibranch
Also called sea slugs, these colourful ocean creatures are distant relatives of land snails. They have a shell for only the first stage of life, and then as adults, emerge as vibrant predators that eat sponges and assorted jellies, corals and shellfish. Denuded of their hard armour, the older slugs instead protect themselves with venomous appendages.

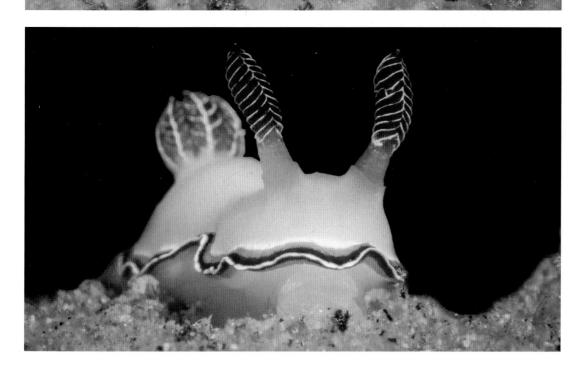

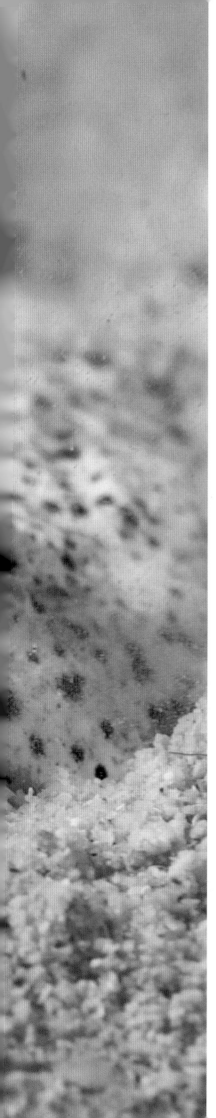

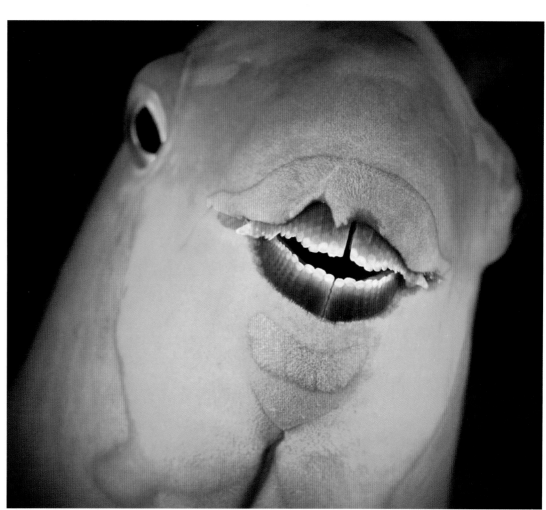

LEFT:

Stargazer

This flatfish is always looking up, lying hidden in the seabed sediment for smaller fish to come by. The stargazer then snatches them up with its wide mouth. As the fish is busy searching for food it is protected by venomous spines behind the head that fend off attack from above.

ABOVE BOTH PHOTOGRAPHS:

Parrotfish

These colourful reef fish use their beak-like mouths to scrape away at corals and rocks. In the process of scooping up the algae that grows there, they also swallow some rocky material, which is pooped out as a fine coral sand.

BOTH PHOTOGRAPHS:

Peacock mantis shrimp

Growing to 18 cm (7 in) long, this is one of the larger mantis shrimps, so named because it uses its front legs to smash, stun or grab prey (a bit like their insect namesakes). Mantis shrimps have perhaps the most acute eyesight in the oceans. Each eye has 10,000 receptors that can detect 12 colour channels and UV light, whereas human eyes see just three colours.

Picture Credits